Understanding Charles Dic

A complete GCSE Study Gui
boards in 2019 and beyond

By Gavin Smithers

Another of Gavin's Guides- study books packed with insight. They aim to help you raise your grade!

Understanding Charles Dickens' "A Christmas Carol" is a complete study guide and is written for both students aiming to achieve the higher grades, and their teachers, as they prepare for GCSE examinations with any of the UK exam boards in Summer 2019 and beyond.

Series Editor: Gill Chilton

Published by Gavin's Guides

All rights reserved. No part of this publication may be reproduced or transmitted in any form or by any means, electronic or mechanical, including photocopy, recording or any information storage and retrieval system, without the prior permission of the publisher.

Copyright Gavin Smithers 2019 . The right of Gavin Smithers to be identified as the author of this work has been asserted in accordance with the Copyright, Designs and Patents Act 1988. This book is copyright material and must not be copied, reproduced, transferred, distributed, leased, licensed or publicly performed or used in any way except as specifically permitted in writing by the publishers, as allowed under the terms and conditions under which it was purchased or as strictly permitted by applicable copyright law. Any unauthorized distribution or use of this text may be a direct infringement of the author's and publisher's rights and those responsible may be liable in law accordingly.

The complete text of "A Christmas Carol" is widely available. You will need a copy to use alongside this study guide.

Understanding Charles Dickens' "A Christmas Carol"

Contents

Let's get started .... page 3

Introduction and the ethos of the novella .. page 7

Your exam board and its requirements ..... page 15

AQA .... page 15

Edexcel .... page 18

WJEC .... page 20

The Characters:

Ebenezer Scrooge.............................page 21

Narrator ....page 33

Marley's Ghost ....page 36

The Ghost of Christmas Past ....page 42

The Ghost of Christmas Present ....page 44

The Ghost of Christmas Yet to Come ....page 47

Bob Cratchit ....page 49

The Cratchit Family ....page 50

The Fezziwigs ....page 53

Fred ....page 55

Belle ....page 58

Narrative Structure – the Scenes .... page 59

Stave 1 .... page 61

Stave 2 .... page 62

Stave 3 .... page 63

Stave 4 .... page 64

Stave 5 .... page 65

Dickens' Use of Comedy .... page 66

Dickens' Use of Pathos .... page 69

The Gothic Element .... page 73

Poverty in the 1840's .... page 75

Scrooge's Timeline .... page 77

The Essays:

Essay 1 .... page 79

Essay 2 .... page 85

Final Tips .... page 91

Let's get started

Dickens' "A Christmas Carol" has been a favourite GCSE text for many years. It's easy to see why; it is a novella (a short novel) which the wider reading public all over the world has always appreciated. It captures the warmth of Christmas while it also confronts us with the reality of child poverty, and asks us uncomfortable questions about the gap between the very poor and the better off.

We think of Christmas as a time when magical or miraculous things can happen and we watch Scrooge transformed from a mean spirited, unhappy antisocial miser into a popular, generous and happy citizen, respected in his local community. Apart from a cast of living human characters, both young and old, it features a ghost and three Spirits, and a strange pair of half-wild children called Ignorance and Want.

This unusual cast list raises questions about why they are included. The plot itself is fairly straightforward- Scrooge is taken from the present to the past, the present again, and the future, then back to the present, to learn from his mistakes and become a different, kinder person.

Dickens uses Scrooge's interactions with the other characters to develop ideas and themes about vulnerability- to greed or poverty or exploitation or lack of opportunity. It is not just an entertaining story, but one with some depth. You will need to show that you understand these issues, and be able to support your arguments about the meaning of the novella with solid evidence and thoughtful analysis. That's where this study guide comes in- it examines themes, contexts and meanings in enough depth to help you to reach into the upper grades, and it will prompt you to think about the other texts you read in the same attentive and thoughtful way.

In this guide, I aim to give you a secure understanding of how Dickens writes, as well as the background context you need.

All examination boards are looking for the same elements in your answer-

1 Evidence that you are familiar with the plot and characters

2 Proof that you can analyse your own feelings and responses as you read

3 The ability to explain how Dickens manages or manipulates our reactions

This guide addresses all of those aspects of the novella, as well as the historical background. Understanding this context (and the Biblical references Dickens chooses to include) helps us to see very clearly what the meaning or message of the story is intended to be.

Read this guide and you will understand clearly what Dickens wanted to say (and why) when he wrote "A Christmas Carol". It will also help you to improve your essay technique.

For GSCE, it is not enough to know what happens in a text. You need to be alert to the "why" and "how" of the writer's creating of the text. That includes being able to connect and relate events which take place several scenes apart; I highlight these connections for you.

So, to deepen your understanding, all you need is a few clear hours…..and the willingness to begin with an open, curious mind.

This short interpretative guide is intended as a supplement to your lessons at school- not a substitute for them. To benefit most, you will need to have read the novella for yourself, all the way through, before you read the critical analysis you will find here.

You may be interested in watching stage or film versions of the story. As with other GCSE texts, a stage version may be appearing in a theatre near you. Check whether a school trip is possible. But remember that a stage version will be a short form featuring the highlights- much has to be left out, so you need to know the written text thoroughly and rely mainly on that. While a play or adaptation can afford to leave out some characters and some of the action, you, when gathering the material to write your exam essay, can't do that!! Yours is a literature exam, not a media studies one.

I am a private tutor in Chipping Campden in Gloucestershire. This book was written initially to help my students. In the same way I help them to achieve higher grades, I hope this will help you. And here's an offer and a promise to back that up………..if you have questions and your teachers can't help, e-mail me and I'll write back with answers. You can contact me at grnsmithers@hotmail.co.uk.

Now let's get to work. Have your copy of the novella to hand, and make notes as you go along. I hope you enjoy exploring Dickens' story as much as I have.

Introduction, and the ethos of the novella

Dickens was born in 1812. His first published stories appeared in 1833. From 1837 onwards he wrote a stream of novels, became a public figure, giving speeches on various issues, and later became a newspaper publisher as well as being involved in charitable work, acting and giving public readings of his own work. He died in 1870, at the age of 58, after suffering a stroke.

He is best known now for his long novels, but "A Christmas Carol", which he wrote quite early in his career (it was published in 1843) set a very popular trend for Christmas books written by him. It sold 5000 copies in its first week, because Dickens was already established as an important and very popular writer.

The background to the tale of Scrooge's redemption is a lively sense in English society that, at a time of economic hardship and economic distress for many people, but not the affluent classes (in the "hungry Forties"), Christmas offers an ideal opportunity to be charitable; the better- off can not only celebrate the festival with their families but can, and should, support poor families who live nearby or are otherwise known to them.

This explains the arrival in Scrooge's office of the two portly gentlemen who are seeking relief for the poor through financial donations from the business community- a little like the Rotary Club today, or, more broadly, Children In Need.

The first Christmas edition of the magazine Punch, in 1841, had criticised insular middle-class overindulgence which ignored the poor, and the first Christmas card, which appeared in 1843, took up the same theme. Perhaps the emergence of a new professional middle class was accompanied by a sense that being poor was still not so far away; the Cratchits are poor by modern standards (they pawn their possessions for short-term credit from time to time, which is like taking out a payday loan today) but they are respectable, and not really poor, in comparison with many of their unskilled contemporaries; Martha works, and Peter will too. They lack education but not the capacity for employment.

Among the most memorable scenes in the novella are Fezziwig's festivities, which include his apprentices, his housemaid, the baker, the cook and the milkman, and "the boy from over the way"; and the Cratchits' very limited, but genial and gracious Christmas, overshadowed by the disability and illness of Tiny Tim. Scrooge's nephew Fred is a determined and hospitable host who resolves not to let his uncle's misanthropy prevail. Attitudes to Christmas, and its social function, are at the heart of the novella. It is a time to celebrate extended families, but also a time to show benevolence by giving money so that the poorest can have a better Christmas. Charities such as Crisis still do this today.

In the eighteenth century, landowners had been responsible for supporting the local poor, and the aristocracy would often hold a Christmas party for their many employees and labourers. In metropolitan London, Victorian houses were smaller, and unsuitable for large parties; but Fezziwig has an office party and there is no reason why Scrooge cannot do the same. Perhaps, judging from the final paragraph of the novella, he does- after his tale of repentance comes to an end.

Dickens gives us a strong sense of the right and wrong way to "do" Christmas. Once Scrooge has had his therapy from the ghosts, which "reclaims" him, and frees him from his childhood memories of Christmas as a lonely and miserable time, he becomes as good as anyone at "keeping Christmas well". For Dickens, this means gathering your extended family around you in an atmosphere of bonhomie and determined optimism and gratitude (like the Cratchits), even if you have to stretch the goose with apple sauce and stuffing. For the better off, it also involves going out into the streets, raising money for the poor among the professional classes, and spreading goodwill and good cheer. Eventually, Scrooge is transformed from an anti-social introvert into an outgoing but discreet philanthropist.

It is worth noting that Scrooge (like the author who creates him) is neither a religious zealot nor a class warrior. The "good man" is a social creature, and Scrooge has failed to live up this ideal until it is almost too late in his life. Scrooge's fiancée had rejected him because he had become obsessed with making money; he is marked out for an unmourned and lonely death because he has done nothing to help those he has come into contact with, year after miserly and miserable year. As Marley's ghost says, humanity should be Scrooge's focus- not preserving his fortune and counting it. Fred memorably speaks about the sterility of Scrooge's money, which helps no-one, and gives no satisfaction, although he hopes to wear his uncle down to the point where he may eventually leave Bob Cratchit a legacy of £50.

In (finally) giving Bob a pay rise, and promising to "assist your struggling family", Scrooge becomes, like his nephew, a man who supports the less fortunate in his own social circle- a practical doer of good deeds, and a man to whom others warm, for the first time in his lonely adult life.

This is a question of personal morality, not ideology; therefore, Scrooge does not become a class warrior or a red-blooded revolutionary who seeks to abolish poverty, the workhouses, prisons and the Poor Laws by overturning the existing social structure. In the world of the story, personal/private charity should and must add to and supplement these resources- not take their place. This may seem strange to us, but the workhouses, though harsh, did at least offer some healthcare and some education to those poor enough to be sent there.

Scrooge reforms himself, after learning from the various Ghosts; he then merely seeks to give something back, as Marley and he had both failed to do- until now. For Marley, the lesson came too late. For Scrooge, it comes just in time.

The emphasis on the old songs sung in mining communities, and on traditional food and parlour games, implies that Dickens sees Christmas as a ceasefire in the hard year-long battle for families' financial security, which can cement the social cohesion and traditions which run from the past to the present and the future. This is the new landscape of Scrooge and the Cratchits, the family he adopts as his own.

Dickens gave no fewer than 127 readings or public performances of the novella between 1853 and his death in

1870. The secret of its enduring popularity in his own life time lies in its unthreatening assertion that it is easy- and proper- to do good at Christmas, not because it is a religious obligation or duty, but because it is good for our soul, regenerative, and it takes us back into our younger, more innocent, child-like selves.

As children, we are less attuned to money, materialism and competition, and more aware of our family bonds and the social networks which extend a little beyond them. Life is simpler and we are more generous with our good wishes for others. We become more judgmental and insecure as adults, and thus less comfortable doing what Scrooge is required to do – until the Spirits concentrate his mind on the need to reclaim his moral respectability.

Dickens wrote to a friend that his Christmas books always gave examples of "the Christian virtues" and promoted "Christian precepts"; we may translate this into the sayings "charity begins at home", "do as you would be done by" and "the love of money is the root of all evil".

Note that, if Scrooge fails to learn the lesson of charity, he will not **explicitly** be condemned to some kind of Hell- he will have to wander the Earth like Marley and the other unnamed businessmen, regretting the fact that he can no longer ease the poverty of the living, as he should have done. There is, however, an **implicit** reference, in the text

Peter Cratchit is reading when Scrooge goes back to Bob's house (Mark's Gospel, 9.36) which suggests that if Scrooge fails to help the Cratchits by saving Tiny Tim, he will indeed be damned.

Dickens pointed out that in every one of his Christmas stories "there is an express text preached on......always taken from the lips of Christ". In "A Christmas Carol", it is Matthew 18.2-

"Jesus called a little child to stand among them. "Truly, I tell you," He said, "unless you change and become like little children, you will never enter the kingdom of heaven." "

This is the carrot approach, rather than the stick of damnation! The central importance of Tiny Tim and the horrific figures of Ignorance and Want put the child at the heart of the novella's meaning- as does Scrooge's nostalgia for his own childhood.

In his excellent book, "Dickens' Christmas- a Victorian Celebration" (Frances Lincoln Limited, 2003, ISBN 978-0-7112-3031-6), Simon Callow sheds light on the curious mixture of the Pagan and the Christian in the English concept of Christmas. The Industrial Revolution, with its move from the wide open spaces and the grand houses of the countryside to more cramped urban living spaces, was changing the complexion of Christmas again- and our conception of it is, post-Dickens, different again. We are less keen on chestnuts, blind-man's buff, figs and French plums. Perhaps "A Christmas Carol" owes its enduring popularity to the skill with which Dickens weaves together different strands which matter to him, because of his own experience of poverty as a child-

- the idea that we live in a prosperous country where we can afford to be generous to those less well off than us

-the idea that children denied the basics of education and an adequate standard of living (Ignorance and Want) must be rescued from the workhouse, the coal mine and the chimney

-the belief that the debtor's prison and the workhouse need to be made obsolete by the expansion of schools, better welfare and better wages (this will take some time to achieve)

-the New Testament message that money must be used wisely (1 Timothy) -

"we brought nothing into this world, and it is certain we can carry nothing out……..the love of money is the root of all evil"-

which is precisely the principle for life which Scrooge finally learns.

As the narrator points out, in stave 3, "it is good to be children sometimes", and Scrooge finally becomes the living embodiment of this truth, in his childish enthusiasm for Christmas, which is reminiscent of his old master Fezziwig's.

The style of the narrative is an attractive mixture of the gothic and the comic; dark and light. For a ghost story, it is reassuringly interested in the living, not the dead!

Your exam board and its requirements

AQA exam requirements

This is easily the most popular exam board for UK students, accounting for more than 60% of entries.

Students with AQA will answer a question on "A Christmas Carol" as one half of Paper 1. The Dickens question contributes 30 marks or almost 20% of your overall result. You will be given a short extract to analyse, and the extract will be the starting point for an essay about the novella as a whole. You should spend 50 minutes on this question.

The summer 2017 exam used an extract of 23 lines about the Cratchits' Christmas pudding, and then asked you to "explore how Dickens uses the Cratchit family to show the struggles of the poor", with the helpful suggestion that your essay should examine how the Cratchits are presented here and how they illustrate or represent the struggles of the poor in the whole novel.

We can break the marking down further. It equates to a maximum of 12 marks for AO1 (demonstrating an informed personal response, and writing in a critical style, using references and quotations to support and explain your views): 12 marks for AO2 (analysing language, form and structure for the meanings and effects they create, and using relevant terminology): and 6 marks for AO3 (showing how the contexts in which the novella was written has influenced or shaped the text).

The mark scheme enables markers to put essay answers into one of the levels 1-6, depending on how well these skills are developed.

The examiners' report on the AQA website is a valuable resource for teachers and candidates. It indicates that understanding how all the parts of the text link with its overall themes is important; that context can be interpreted as a question of the way literary forms/genres work, both historically, and as this applies to us today, but that the details of Dickens' own life are not very relevant to the exam.

A tip here for those of you seeking top grades is to start with the text as a whole and then "dip in and out" of the extract and the whole text, rather than start with a detailed analysis of the extract. The reason for this is that it encourages you to show that you have a settled and broadly based understanding of the whole novella. Using many quotations will not get you extra marks- references are not defined just as quotations, but as pointers and paraphrases too.

The report makes the point that characters are constructed to serve a particular purpose- for example, the Cratchits are an archetypal upper working class family. They are by no means the poorest family, but they are honest strivers who deserve an easier life. Scrooge and Fred have the opportunity to help them. Fred sees it as a pleasure and a duty, and Scrooge belatedly learns this for himself.

Both Mrs Cratchit and Fred's wife criticise Scrooge for his lack of care; they are right to do so. Their husbands refuse to make the same biting personal criticisms of Scrooge. The two husbands are probably less resentful and judgmental, and more resilient, because they work in a wider world outside the home where they see all kinds of injustices being done to all kinds of poor people. Bob writes letters which bear down, on Scrooge's behalf, on those poorer than himself.

You will be rewarded for explaining what Dickens does with his characters.

The AQA examiners' report for 2017 ends with seven bullet points. As well as expected advice – know your text, read the question accurately – the report also has these tips: appreciate big themes and ideas and, whilst it is good to analyse the language the writer uses, remember too that analysing structure and characterisation are also key.

There is also a specimen question on Scrooge that you might want to study. Additionally, further on in this Gavin's Guide, I have two further essays that I have written to give a flavour of how an essay following all their guidelines might read. (Page XX).

Edexcel exam requirements

Your question on this text is in Paper 2; you will also be writing about your poetry studies (the anthology, and unseen poetry). **You are advised to spend 55 minutes on "A Christmas Carol".**

The question is divided into two equally weighted parts. First, there is an extract in which you will be invited to "explore how Dickens presents" a character or theme (in

2017, the children Ignorance and Want); then you will be asked to explain how that theme or character is portrayed or presented in the novel as a whole.

This question is assessed equally on AO1 and AO2. You are rewarded/assessed for giving an informed or defensible personal response, which you support with references from the text, and writing in a suitable critical style (AO1); and for analysing how language, form and structure create meanings and effects. You are not marked on your awareness of context.

The examiners' report comments on the need/opportunity to write about "the moral meaning" of the text and the "hidden meaning" of the child-figures in the extract- a useful reminder that the story presents itself as an oral ghost tale, but is in fact a carefully constructed **representation**, designed to be **a platform for serious questions about the values of society in the reader's own time**. Since poverty continues to be a social issue (politicians are forever talking about the benefits system, and the virtues of getting the poor into paid work) it is clear that it has not lost any of its relevance, even today.

The report includes two exam responses. Neither of them makes the link between the contrasting opportunities "little Fan" and "Tiny Tim" have, and the difference some education and some financial security makes to a child's resilience, happiness and prospects. Dickens draws both characters in order to attach a sense of pathos to Tiny Tim. The family which can afford to educate its son (Scrooge) at boarding school is not like the Cratchits (or the Gargerys in "Great Expectations") and it can be supposed to have an income of more than 15 shillings per week.

WJEC requirements

The novella is an option in Unit 2b. Here you will have an hour to answer a question in two parts- a twenty minute analysis of how Dickens creates "mood and atmosphere", and a forty minute essay on a theme or a character (in 2017, the theme was responsibility and the character Bob Cratchit).

The essay questions explored here serve as models for WJEC too.

Because, regardless of which exam board you are with, your exam question is very likely to be about characters and themes, and not so much about being able to recite the plot, let's take a deeper look now into these characters and themes. I think you will find it helpful to see the plot as a series of "scenes"- you can imagine them unfolding on the stage in the theatre- and I list those separate scenes later in this guide

The Characters

Ebenezer Scrooge

Scrooge starts the novella as a man with whom we have no sympathy. It becomes clear, early on, that what he says, and how he says it, both indicate that he has a mean and passive-aggressive character. He is set in his unpleasant ways. He is deeply anti-social; his one wish is "to be left alone".

In Stave 1, we find out that he is unsentimental- he went straight back to work after Marley's funeral (this Christmas Eve is the seventh anniversary of Marley's death). He did not remove Marley's name from his business, even though he might be mistaken for Marley; this implies an absence of personal vanity, and also that Marley was his alter ego- they were/are very alike in their values and preoccupations (making money and keeping it to themselves).

The narrator labels Scrooge as "tight-fisted......grasping......covetous old sinner.....hard....secret, and self-contained, and solitary as an oyster"; his lips are thin, he has "ferret eyes" and his voice grates. As sinners go, he is a skilled one; this introduction leaves us in no doubt that he is morally in the wrong.

He emits not warmth but cold. His emotional temperature never changes, the narrator observes, because he is unaffected by changes in the weather. The term "sinner" is interesting because it implies that we will witness Scrooge's belated repentance and redemption. The spirits show him uncomfortable truths and the opportunities to live a good life which he has refused to take. Although the narrative does not show Scrooge confessing his sins or asking for forgiveness (from God) it has the same cleansing or purifying effect; as with giving up smoking, it seems that, to improve your health, it is never too late to give up being miserly and unpleasant to people.

The comment that he was not "open to entreaty", together with the appearance of the debtors Caroline and her husband in stave 4, suggests that Scrooge is a pitiless moneylender, although he trades from a "warehouse" which is really an office. Presumably the letters Bob Cratchit writes are letters collecting money from his clients.

Scrooge, according to the narrator, repels people; they will not ask him for help or directions, and even guide dogs for the blind go out of the way to avoid him. This unpleasant, repulsive aura is neatly reversed at the end of the novella, where Scrooge walks around with "a delighted smile" and is "so irresistibly pleasant" that people greet him in the street spontaneously.

In stave 1, Scrooge gives Fred a morose definition of Christmas as "a time for finding yourself a year older and not an hour richer", and he equates happiness with wealth, saying that the poor have no right to be merry. He expresses his hostility to the concept of greeting people with the words "Merry Christmas", and he himself sticks instead to the unseasonal "Good afternoon" as his Christmas greeting.

He has no answer, when Fred asks him why he is rich and miserable; he is not quick-witted, or especially intelligent, but he has a rich store of sarcastic remarks- suggesting that Fred should become an MP, because he has so much to say about society, and pretending that if charity is needed from private citizens the prisons and workhouses must have closed down. He is a man of no imagination, or "what is called fancy".

Scrooge speaks "sternly" and "indignantly"; he "growls" and "mutters", "demands" and "frowns". He refuses to explain his attitude to Fred, and gets rid of him by closing the conversation with five repetitions of "Good afternoon!". This is called "the broken record technique"- simply saying the same thing over and over again, until the person you say it to eventually gives up the attempt to engage you in a conversation.

Scrooge says that if poor people will not go to the prisons or the workhouse they should "die…..and decrease the surplus population"- a view which the Ghost of Christmas Present in stave 3 rams forcefully down Scrooge's throat, when they discuss the fate of Tiny Tim; Scrooge then hears his own words "with penitence and grief", because his humanity is thawing out, and he knows that his lack of empathy has cost him, not money, but a great deal of lost happiness.

He defines his philosophy as minding his own business, "and not to interfere with other people's". He sends the carol-singing boy away "in terror". He is reluctant to shut up shop on the evening of Christmas Eve ("ill-will……walked out with a growl"). He treats it exactly the same as any other day- he goes to a pub for his usual "melancholy dinner", reads the newspapers, reads his bank statements, and goes home.

Our first impressions of Scrooge come from how he speaks to Fred, the two portly gentlemen, and Bob Cratchit. He resents paying Bob, and he resents the expense of fuel; his home is surrounded by offices (a symbol of his interest only in work, and not in leisure or outside interests), and money is his constant preoccupation. Dickens further characterises Scrooge by attaching the language of gloom and cold to him. It is as if his emotional coldness spreads outwards so that other people feel it- the ice is described as "misanthropic", an adjective (transferred epithet) which applies in fact to Scrooge.

His approach to life is summed up in his motto "Bah! Humbug!" and his frustrated comment to Fred that he lives in "such a world of fools". Hard, sharp and cold, he does not believe in anything warm or soft; he is arrogant in his "improved opinion of himself" and he almost becomes angry over the issue of charity for the poor (from whom he himself appears to profit). If he is a moneylender, or a payday lender, then he will not want to see the poor better off, because he makes a living from their lack of financial security.

Seeing Marley's face in the doorknocker leaves him "startled", but he does not believe in the supernatural, so he refuses "to be frightened by echoes". When the bell in the house starts ringing he feels "great astonishment……..a strange, inexplicable dread", and he is slow to accept that Marley's ghost is real; his rationality allows humour to creep into his dialogue here. He remains outwardly calm, but experiences "terror….horror"; when the ghost removes its bandage and its jaw drops, Scrooge "fell upon his knees", recognising that he is dealing with the supernatural. He begins to have physical reactions to the ghost and its message- "trembling………trembled more and more…….began to quake exceedingly……..shivered"; he becomes "desperate in his curiosity" and he seems open-minded to the ghost's description of life after death, in a form of purgatory, for those who could have made the world a happier place but chose not to.

By the end of Stave 1, Scrooge has lost some of his scepticism and certainty, so that he cannot say "Humbug!" with conviction. He has been asking Marley's ghost questions "in a faultering voice", and he deserves credit for being quick to "apply to himself" what Marley's ghost says about wasted opportunities to use properly our "vast means of usefulness". He understands that there is a difference between being "a good man of business" or even "a good friend" and being a force "for good, in human matters". The insight is the need to align what you think of as good for yourself with what is good for other people.

At the end of Stave 1. Scrooge's lifelong certainties have been shaken, and his "humility and deference" are such that we begin to feel a little less cold towards him. The narrator's early judgments about Scrooge have receded as the pace of the narrative picks up, too, so that we feel he is more vulnerable and therefore less repellent.

Stave 2 promotes a more generous view of Scrooge, because he is now subject to dramatic irony- like a tragic hero, he cannot make sense of his experience with the ghost of Marley, but the reader can.

Scrooge does not greet the Ghost of Christmas Past rudely, or in terror, but politely. He expresses his vulnerability ("I am a mortal……..and liable to fall"). Transported to his childhood, the emotions he has repressed as a solitary, misanthropic adult start to come out- "a thousand thoughts, and hopes, and joys, and cares, long, long forgotten!"- and prompt him to tears which he will not acknowledge. His feelings are "fervour……gladness" but at school he was "a lonely boy", sent to boarding school by an unfeeling father and left there, the only pupil, in the Christmas holidays.

Reading was his imaginative escape, and recalling this makes Scrooge expressive and animated; he is becoming a child again, emotionally. He feels "pity for his former self", the first step towards feeling compassion for others in the present and the future.

His compassion for boys such as him makes him think of the carol singer he had sent away in terror, and foreshadows his much more appreciative and generous treatment of the turkey-fetching boy in Stave 5; a sense of personal guilt and of lost time motivates his philanthropy.

Confronted with the memory of his dead sister, Scrooge also feels "uneasy in his mind" over his unfriendliness to his nephew, Fred.

We are conscious of the contrast between Fezziwig's treatment of Scrooge (as his employee and apprentice), giving him a celebratory Christmas, and Scrooge's treatment of Bob Cratchit. Scrooge experiences "the strangest agitation" because this is a memory of a Happy or Merry Christmas; he has since persuaded himself that such merriment is of no value, but Fezziwig's example is one he could- and should- follow. He realises that he has mistreated Bob- as with the carol-singer, and Fred, Scrooge can now see how he may correct his past mistakes and do better in the future.

In the scene in which his fiancée breaks off their engagement, observing that he has become devoted, instead of to her, to "Gain", Scrooge is passive, as he is judged unfavourably. He then has to witness his former fiancée enjoying a domestic life "full of comfort" and laughter, with a husband, and children, on the day of Marley's death (seven years ago), while Scrooge is observed as being "Quite alone in the world", so that he now faces "the haggard winter of his life". The room concerned (which stands for the house, and for her whole way of life) is "not very large or handsome, but full of comfort"- unlike Scrooge's ice-cold office and house.

In Stave 2, Scrooge has found the Ghost's light- the light of enlightenment or truth- painful, because it has shown him that his experience of Christmas has not been all bad; that he should be enhancing the happiness of those people in his world; and that his isolation is entirely self-willed and self-imposed. The ghost has shown him that actions have consequences, and that perceiving ourselves as victims, and being passive and isolated, does not excuse us from our social duty. There is always the choice to see ourselves and our world differently.

The sense that Scrooge's past has been a succession of painful emotional failures means that we now empathise with him considerably more. We have understood that the ghosts' mission is Scrooge's "welfare" and "reclamation"- he needs to be deconstructed and then reassembled as a feeling, functioning human being. His willingness to undergo the pain involved in this drawn-out process is brave. He was not altogether joking when he had asked Marley's ghost whether he could not "take 'em all at once, and have it over, Jacob?" He is suffering his purgatory in life so that he can avoid it in death. Perhaps his transformation is a little like that of Frankenstein, with Marley designing the superior or at least improved being

Scrooge becomes. He is re-engineered as thoroughly "good" in all regards by the end of the tale.

At the start of Stave 3, Scrooge proactively pulls his bed-curtains aside; he is almost welcoming the next Spirit, and wants to avoid "surprise and being made nervous". It is a "jolly Giant" but Scrooge is now humbler than he used to be; he speaks "reverently………..submissively" and distinguishes between the lessons he has learnt from the Ghost of Christmas Past, "on compulsion", and his willingness to learn from this new Spirit, who dispenses friendliness and bonhomie.

Scrooge's observation of the Cratchits' Christmas makes him especially interested in what will happen to Tiny Tim ("with an interest he had never felt before"); he is confronted with his previous lack of compassion for the weakest members of society, who, he had said, were welcome to die "and decrease the surplus population". Scrooge learns that, unless he behaves differently, Tiny Tim will die within twelve months. He also sees and hears Mrs Cratchit's hostility- she complains that he has given them nothing, and is "Baleful….the Ogre". Scrooge has now learnt the harsh lesson that no life is worth less than another; this prompts his new concern for the Cratchits, whose poverty lays them open to illness and death- especially Tiny Tim.

He hears himself being discussed among Fred's family, as "not so pleasant…..a bear….the old man", and hears Fred's argument that he is only making himself more miserable. The Spirit "taught Scrooge his precepts"- that in any place, however harsh, people are saying "a kinder word….than on any day in the year; and had shared to some extent in its festivities". Everyone, including those whose lives are harsher than his, is celebrating Christmas with a generous spirit- with the sole exception of Scrooge. The Ghost of Christmas Present confronts him with the disturbing and morally offensive figures of Want and Ignorance; Scrooge is "appalled", and he is warned not to ignore the needs of children, and that his former belief- that prisons and workhouses are adequate to house the poor- is wrong, because the lasting cure for poverty is education and knowledge. Scrooge does not resist what he is shown; he absorbs it and takes it to heart. Our hostility to him has more or less come to an end, by the end of Stave 3.

In Stave 4, Scrooge has to answer his own questions, because the Ghost of Christmas Yet To Come is silent. The forbidding Ghost induces in him fear, trembling, shuddering, a very cold feeling and "a vague uncertain horror" because he is being seen by it but cannot see any of it, beyond its hand and its black clothing. The tour the Ghost takes him on includes the Exchange, other business premises he used to frequent, the dingy place where his personal belongings are sold on, his own corpse, debtors for whom his death is a relief, and his own tombstone. Scrooge can infer that he is likely to be unmissed and unmourned unless he changes his way of life.

When he begs the Ghost to "let me see some tenderness connected with a death", he sees the Cratchits, minus Tiny Tim, who has just died, and the focus is (tellingly) on "the extraordinary kindness of Mr Scrooge's nephew", with his empathy for the bereaved. Fred has offered to help the Cratchits, although he hardly knows them. Scrooge has not, although he sees Bob all day, every day.

Stave 4 is the darkest and most gothic part of the narrative, after which all is sunshine and light in Stave 5. Scrooge is a reformed character, "glowing with his good intentions" because of his relief at having the opportunity to avoid the fate he has been shown. His simultaneous "laughing and crying" is the same response as when he revisited his childhood innocence; he now dispenses "merry Christmas to everybody" instead of "Bah! Humbug!"; he laughs with the same enthusiasm as his nephew and his happy household.

The verbs which denote Scrooge's movement- "frisked, running, rubbing his hands, splitting with a laugh, dance, leaping, clapped him on the back, chuckled, laughed"- dramatize the pleasure Scrooge now takes in his own "alteration" to a kind of Fezziwig figure. His speech is generous, complimentary and constructive- in Stave 1, he would never have used words like "delightful…pleasure…..wonderful….pardon….goodness…favour….bless……my friend".

The old Scrooge thought it was a mad idea that a family as poor as the Cratchits could have a merry Christmas ("I'll retire to Bedlam"); but now Bob thinks Scrooge has gone mad, when he gives him a pay rise ("he had a momentary idea of….calling…..for help and a strait-waistcoat").

Scrooge is a completely reformed character. In what he does and what he says, warmth has replaced coldness, and his generosity brings with it a level of happiness worth much more than the cost of the pay rise he gives Bob, his donation to charity, and the price of a large turkey.

The narrator

The novella is a third-person narrative, but Dickens deploys a narrator to give the impression that this- like the most effective ghost stories- is being spoken to us, rather than merely read ("the story I am going to relate"). The presence of the narrator is established in the opening paragraphs, where he(she?) muses on the peculiarity of the expression "as dead as a doornail", and observes that "as dead as a coffin nail" might be more accurate.

The narrator is familiar with Shakespeare's play "Hamlet", and he assumes the listener is, too.

His usefulness lies in the way he can define Scrooge's character and behaviour for us before we encounter Scrooge for ourselves; until the dialogue with Fred begins, we are reading an introductory exposition which establishes the tone of the tale and gives us a sense of Scrooge's appearance and personality.

We are less conscious of the narrator's role or presence (it's a bit ghostly!) once the action develops in the succession of scenes in different locations. He asserts himself again when he describes the width of the staircase in Scrooge's house ("I mean to say you might have got a hearse up that staircase……."). Early in Stave 2, the narrator is the means of the surreal joke "The Spirit must have heard him thinking…" and of more extended humour over Scrooge's head cold, which he might have used as an excuse not to go out in the wintry night with the Ghost.

Near the end of Stave 2, the narrator intervenes in the description of Scrooge's former fiancée Belle's happy home- "What would I not have given to be one of them!"- and he stresses her physical attractiveness.

He pops up again in the second paragraph of Stage 3- "I don't mind calling on you to believe that he was ready for a good broad field of strange appearances", with a touch of humour- and goes on to say that Scrooge "began to think- as you or I would have thought at first", a way of positioning himself and the reader/listener as quicker on the uptake than the protagonist.

He delivers a further comic nudge over the Cratchits' Christmas dinner- "you might have thought a goose the rarest of all birds; a feathered phenomenon"; but he also delivers an important judgement which guides us in our opinion of the family, and directs our sympathy towards them- in the paragraph which begins "they were not a handsome family………".

In the scene at Fred's house, the narrator provides a flourish to emphasise Fred's good humour ("if you should happen, by any unlikely chance, to know a man more blest………..all I can say is, I should like to know him too. Introduce him to me"). As with Belle, he lingers in a description of Fred's wife ("She was very pretty…..").

He passes the authorial/moral judgment that "it is good to be children sometimes, and never better than at Christmas, when its mighty Founder was a child himself." He pretends to be outraged at Topper's pursuit of "that plump sister" in the game of blind-man's buff. The narrator's benevolence and approval of pleasure allies him with the Ghost of Christmas Present.

The narrator's appreciation of other people's good humour surfaces in some of the description of Scrooge in the closing pages; he uses the word "chuckle(d)" six times in five lines (repetition for emphasis) and observes that Scrooge might have "cut the end of his nose off" without losing his new-found bonhomie. The narrator is alert to opportunities to inject physical comedy into the tale as he tells it.

The final two paragraphs are the narrator's. He uses the adjective "good" seven times, along with the comparative "better" and the adverbial "infinitely more"; he deploys laugh/laughed/ laughter/laughed; and he stresses that "Tiny Tim …did NOT die", and that Scrooge is a "man alive".

The narrator does not slow the narrative down. His(her?) persona is that of someone who agrees with the thesis of the tale- that we have a duty to spread happiness at Christmas. He is a bon viveur himself, appreciative of jokes, the power of female attraction, an enthusiast for the playful and the childlike, but with some moral seriousness. He helps to defuse the darker, gothic elements which necessarily accompany the ghosts, and he always nudges the tale in the direction of redemptive humour rather than fear and sermonising. If we were inclined to freeze with fear, as Scrooge does, when the first Spirit appears, the narrator makes that impossible, in telling us that when Scrooge was "face to face with the unearthly visitor", he was "as close to it as I am now to you, and I am standing in the spirit at your elbow".

Marley's Ghost

Marley's Ghost only appears once, on the seventh anniversary of his death. His dialogue with Scrooge clarifies the premise of the story- that the love of money is a distraction, responsible for much of the grinding poverty which afflicts society and which tests the resilience of families like the Cratchits so sorely.

Marley's face in the door knocker is "not angry or ferocious"; its hair looks agitated by "hot-air"; its eyes are staring and it glows in the dark, and it has no personal desire to haunt Scrooge but is subject to a mission "beyond its control". The ghost itself merits only a short description; the important details are the chain it wears, "long………made…of cash-boxes, keys, padlocks, ledgers, deeds and heavy purses wrought in steel"- all the paraphernalia of Scrooge's life- and the "wrapper" which stops its lower jaw from falling on to its chest.

This "wrapper" or bandage is a telling, carefully selected detail which makes the ghost frightful. Dickens delays it until after he has made a joke about ghosts being see-through, and Marley having "no bowels" (in the double meaning of intestines and compassion). The ghost is presented in suitable Gothic language (bristling, death-cold, chilling...fixed, glazed eyes, very awful, infernal, frightful cry, dismal and appalling noise, horror, clanked...hideously, dead silence, you will be haunted, sounds of lamentation, wailings, moaning) but the conversation with Scrooge is less ominous. Scrooge speaks to the ghost "with humility and deference", but very much as if Marley is still alive, and as he was in life.

The ghost emphasises the seriousness of Scrooge's situation and shows him, in the form of the crowd of ghosts outside the window at the end of Stave 1, the consequences of ignoring his challenge- being miserable for ever because, in death, he will have "lost the power for ever.....to interfere, for good, in human matters".

As a favour to Scrooge, the ghost has arranged "a chance and hope of escaping my fate" (wandering the earth, witnessing the lost and neglected opportunities to foster "happiness", unable to rest....stay...linger anywhere). He says that any individual, "any Christian spirit", has the capacity to be hugely "useful", by concentrating on "charity, mercy, forbearance, and benevolence", and visiting the poor. Scrooge can avoid the ghost's "penance" in the afterlife by starting to do what he should have been doing for the whole of his adult lifetime.

The ghost explains that Scrooge will be haunted or visited by "Three Spirits" in succession, although he does not specify what they represent. The dialogue becomes more severe and serious- to begin with, Scrooge had wondered if a ghost, having no physical substance, could sit on a chair, and he told the ghost off, jokily, for not focusing its look on the toothpick. Their dialogue has been polite, and featured taking turns to speak, as if it were a normal conversation; the fact that one of the speakers is dead makes this comical. Scrooge's scepticism wears off, until he concedes that he must accept that ghosts do exist after all. From that point, the ghost can explain its misery and the reasons for it.

Dickens uses Marley's ghost to position the plot, and to establish the tone of the narrative, in which the balance between the ghostly/gothic/ retributive and the humorous/ redemptive leans towards the second- the mood is more optimistic and forward-looking than gloomy.

The Ghost of Christmas Past

This ghost appears as a hand and a flash of light. It is described as "strange" and contradictory- like a child, and like an old man shrunken to the size of a child (because it can unlock the whole of a life, from childhood memories to old age). Its hair is the white hair of old age, but its face is wrinkle-free. Its arms and hands are very strong, because, as it does to Scrooge in the last scene of Stave 2, it sometimes has to use physical force to make people confront unpleasant aspects of their own past. It is dressed in white, decorated with summer flowers and carrying holly (meaning that it encompasses all times of year). Most significantly, "from the crown of its head there sprung a bright clear jet of light". This is *symbolic*- the Ghost will bring **enlightenment, expose secrets to the light, and shed light** on Scrooge's hatred of Christmas (which derives from his own lonely childhood Christmases).

In case this description makes the Ghost too like a normal human being, Dickens adds some surreal details- the "figure" can be light or dark, distinct or unclear, have a varying number of arms and legs, have a head or be headless.

Its voice is "soft and gentle. Singularly low". This is an echo or intertextual reference to Shakespeare's "King Lear"; there, the redemptive Cordelia's voice was "ever soft, gentle and low". The effect is that readers of Shakespeare (and remember the allusion to "Hamlet" in the opening paragraphs in Stave 1) will understand that the Ghost is a force for good in a confused world which has lost its sense of moral values.

The Ghost clarifies for Scrooge that he is the ghost of Scrooge's own past- hence the child/old man doubling up, and the white hair. He tells Scrooge that he has come to help with his "welfare" or "reclamation"- to rescue him from the consequences of his past choice, of his own free will, to use his life only to pursue money (like Marley).

The Ghost's instruction to Scrooge, "Rise! And walk with me!" is virtually a quotation of Christ's words in St John 5:8- "Rise, take up thy bed, and walk". This relates a miracle where a man who had been crippled for 38 years was instantly cured- it hints at the sudden and complete transformation the ghosts will make of Scrooge.

As the Ghost takes Scrooge on a tour of his younger days, the focus is on what Scrooge sees, and his reactions; so the Ghost has relatively little to say, and that is mostly linking the separate scenes or memories, acting as a bridge between them. Its touch is gentle, its manner thoughtful. At the Fezziwig scene, "the light upon its head burnt very clear", because the Ghost makes the important point- enlightening Scrooge- that creating happiness need not cost much money.

When Scrooge realises that his love of making money has been at the expense of his personal happiness, and he shrinks from the "torture" of being shown the life he could have had, "the relentless Ghost pinioned him in both of his arms, and forced him to observe". The Ghost will not be deflected from its serious purpose here. The scenes it shows Scrooge induce guilt, embarrassment, and a sense of failure- all of which are necessary before someone can really commit themselves in a highly motivated way to living the rest of their life differently. Scrooge experiences distress and "a struggle", in coming to terms with his suppressed sense of failure; at the moment where he realises how wrong he has been about so many things, the Ghost's "light was burning high and bright". In making Scrooge confront all of his past life, the Ghost has freed him and performed a service rather like psychotherapy.

The Ghost of Christmas Present

This ghost is more solid and recognisable human than the previous two- it is a party-loving "jolly Giant, glorious to see", dressed in dark green, like a folklore forest king. It, too, emits light, but this light is red and warm ("a blaze of ruddy light") and it comes from the "glowing torch" it carries. The Ghost introduces himself and speaks to Scrooge in a friendly way, with a "clear and kind" expression in its eyes. Its manner reflects its character- "genial, sparkling, open, cheery, unconstrained, joyful". Again (as with the money belt Marley's ghost wore as a defining characteristic) this ghost has a trademark detail- a scabbard "eaten up with rust" and without a sword- because it exists to spread harmony and peace at Christmas.

The Ghost's cryptic remark that he has more than eighteen hundred brothers is explained when we understand, at the end of Stave 3, that Christmas Present lasts only for one festive season- so, in the mid- 19th century, more than 1800 of his "elder brothers"- the Christmases of all A.D. previous years- have preceded him.

This Ghost takes Scrooge on a wide-ranging tour which is designed to demonstrate how resilient and humble the poor are. It is as if the Ghost is the patron saint of the poor, sprinkling some badly needed extra good feeling on their limited celebrations. He is outraged by the move by the Sabbatarians to close the bakeries on Sundays and deprive the poor of their only means of having a hot meal once a week.

The adjectives attached to the Ghost continue to define him as a friendly and positive influence- "good, kind, generous, hearty….outpouring, bright, generous"- and he is a particular patron of the Cratchits.

The Ghost's generosity does not extend to Scrooge's harsh past words about the death of the poor serving the social good (because it will "decrease the surplus population")- the Ghost impresses on Scrooge, repeating the phrase, that "If these shadows remain unaltered by the Future" Tiny Tim will die (from poverty). He condemns Scrooge's past, stated view as "wicked cant", and accuses him of arrogance in his opinion that some lives are worth less than others (the lives of the poor being worth less than the lives of the affluent).

The Ghost induces laughter, in the lamplighting boy they pass in the street, at Fred's house, and wherever he goes. He even infects Scrooge with a playful, childlike spirit, so that Scrooge "begged like a boy to be allowed to stay". The Ghost says no; the tour of the nation's poor has to be completed, and they spend the time until Twelfth Night (the end of the Christmas holidays, on 5th January) visiting "misery's every refuge", where the Ghost "left his blessing and taught Scrooge his precepts".

These principles are that the poor are as entitled as the rich to happiness at Christmas, and that the poor must not be ignored or condemned as an inferior social group.

As with the previous ghosts, the Ghost of Christmas Present announces that he has very little time left, and he does something to drive his lesson home, just as Marley's ghost showed Scrooge the misery of the money-minded dead "personally known to Scrooge", and the Ghost of Christmas Past confronted him with his loss of happiness.

This is the dramatic presentation of the allegorical child-figures of Ignorance and Want. The Ghost is especially concerned that Scrooge is aware of Ignorance- his own ignorance/prejudice about the innocence and intrinsic human value of the poor. The allegorical children are emaciated, devilish rather than angelic, and "menacing…….horrible and dread".

The Ghost implies that if the poor continue to be neglected ("unless the writing be erased"), as they have been, by society in general and Scrooge in particular, Ignorance will lead to "Doom"- perhaps a social revolution. His final words to Scrooge dismiss Scrooge's argument that the debtors' prisons and the workhouses are the proper places for the poor. Any sense of "torture" that Scrooge has felt is not comparable with the pain suffered by the invisible millions who are hidden away in "misery's every refuge"- hence

Marley's Ghost's argument that everyone's "business" is charity and benevolence.

The Ghost of Christmas Yet To Come

In a sense, the future is something less tangible for us than the past and the present. Each of the successive phantoms or spirits has had much to show Scrooge, and less to say to him, once the central premise- that he needs to live a different kind of life- is understood.

Scrooge's journey, therefore, is really a quest for him to find the answers to his own questions (he is often puzzled and unable to see why he is being shown a particular scene). The final ghost refuses to answer any questions at all; it merely points with its hand.

Its description belongs to the gothic world of horror. It sees, but it cannot be seen, because it is "shrouded in a deep black garment, which concealed its head, its face, its form". It moves "slowly, gravely, silently". It has "Unseen Eyes". These descriptions are full of the lexis or language of death, and this phantom wants to make Scrooge acutely and painfully aware that no one will miss him, and some people will be relieved at his death- unless he stops being what Marley called him- "a man of the worldly mind".

Contemplating our own death is a sombre business, and Stave 5 is suitably dark and serious. The phantom takes Scrooge to a series of scenes which involve people talking about someone who has died, or where he is/was, dead, or absent, and unmourned - a knot of business men; two business men Scrooge knows; old Joe's shop; his deathbed; his debtors; more resorts of business men; his former office; his grave. At none of these locations does the Ghost speak, but an internal voice is beginning to speak to Scrooge. When he views the corpse (his own), that voice is telling him the difference between good deeds, which soften death by sowing something immortal, and the ruin of the unloved and avaricious.

The question the Ghost's silence asks us is what our "legacy" will be. Scrooge's is to save Tiny Tim from a poverty-induced death by helping the Cratchits financially. Although it does not answer his questions, the Ghost complies with Scrooge's request to take him to see "emotion caused by this man's death", to see "some tenderness connected with a death", and to clarify "what man that was whom we saw lying dead". At his own graveside, Scrooge says what the Ghost would say if it were to speak ("Men's courses will foreshadow certain ends………….."). The fact that Scrooge can now express for himself what the various ghosts had to teach him proves that his transformation is complete. The Ghost's hand shakes and trembles, to confirm to Scrooge that a better end for him is still possible. It then "shrunk, collapsed, and dwindled down" because Scrooge's lesson has been learnt, thoroughly, and late, but not too late.

Scrooge's inability to connect the person spoken of with himself generates dramatic irony- untilhe sees his own gravestone.

Bob Cratchit

Bob works for Scrooge, as his clerk, "copying letters"- a mind-numbing job in a numbingly cold outer office, "a sort of tank", in Scrooge's "counting-house". Scrooge refuses him the small amount of coal he needs to keep warm. He cannot help applauding Fred's injunction to Scrooge to be more cheerful, and then, feeling embarrassed, he accidentally puts his one-coal fire out.

He is paid fifteen shillings a week and he has a wife and a family. When he escapes from the office, he runs home to Camden Town (the run down area of London Dickens had been reduced to living in as a child) after going down a slide twenty times- his enthusiasm for Christmas is like Fred's.

Bob is characterised by his extreme pride in and concern for his family, especially his children. He has no fear of poverty, because he lives in it, and so discredits Scrooge's pathological fear of it. What Bob fears is losing his children to poverty-induced illness- especially the crippled and "feeble" Tiny Tim.

He is "mild", in that he resents no-one else's good fortune or his own lack of security.

The Cratchit family

The Christmas scene at the Cratchit's cramped and poorly equipped home is located more or less centrally in the novella and it is given a long and detailed description.

It is a "four-roomed house", where Bob lives with his wife (who calls him Robert), his daughters Martha and Belinda, and his sons Peter and Tiny Tim, and a younger boy and girl who are not named. Martha appears to have been working overnight on Christmas Eve.

Their clothes are "poor". We already knew that Bob does not have a winter coat to wear to and from the office: his clothes are "thread-bare" and "darned", and his cuffs as "shabby" as they could possibly be.

They cannot afford a turkey, but only a (small and inferior) goose. With it there are mashed potatoes, apple sauce, sage and onion stuffing, and Christmas pudding made with brandy. It is a plain meal, lacking the abundance (of meat and mince pies) at Fezziwig's or the exotic range of fruits, vegetables and fish which Dickens set out immediately before this scene, in his description of what is in the shops.

They drink a solution of hot gin, water and lemon, and have apples, oranges and chestnuts.

Bob proposes a toast to Scrooge, who, as the man who employs him, is "the Founder of the Feast". Mrs Cratchit disagrees- she knows how meagre their Christmas is, and how far from benevolent Scrooge is ("such an odious, stingy, hard, unfeeling man") - but Bob will not have a cross word said in front of the children.

The narrator makes the specific point about the Cratchits that they are poor, but respectable and hard-working, despite their lack of advantages (not a handsome family……not well dressed). But, although they live a hand to mouth existence, they see themselves as a happy family, and as part of a cohesive society- "They were happy, grateful, pleased with one another, and contented with the time".

The Ghost of Christmas Yet To Come takes Scrooge back to "poor" Bob's house. Tiny Tim has died, and, in the absence of Bob, Peter, the oldest boy, reads from the Bible- from Mark's Gospel, 9.36. The following verses in the Bible, which Peter does not read out, make a point which is central to the Christian ethos of the tale, and which explains Scrooge's apparently obsessive, nervous interest in Tiny Tim. These Gospel verses, omitted by Dickens from the scene as Scrooge sees it, and spoken by Jesus, create a context in which Tiny Tim is to be seen as the son of God, and in which anyone who offends a child (or, by implication, fails to help one) will be condemned to Hell. This is the moment of Scrooge's epiphany, where the unspoken threat of damnation emphatically reinforces the social and moral arguments which are about to make Scrooge a truly, permanently reformed character. In case we miss the child/God equation, the narrator exclaims "Tiny Tim, thy childish essence was from God!"

Bob has been out to arrange a burial-plot for Tiny Tim, who lies upstairs, dead- or will die, unless Scrooge deflects the family's poverty; Fred has already offered to help them. Within a couple of pages, Scrooge has sent Bob the turkey, raised his salary and promised to support the "struggling family"; and, in becoming "a second father" to Tim, he learns lasting philanthropy. Because he survives, giving the last words to Tiny Tim ("God Bless Us, Every One!") are an affirmation of Christmas, not the mawkish obituary they might have become if Scrooge were not rescued from his miserly misanthropy.

The Fezziwigs

Fezziwig, like Marley, is dead these days, but Scrooge is excited to be shown the scene of Christmas in the warehouse, by the Ghost of Christmas Past. Where Scrooge's own gestures are crabbed and mean, stiff and grating, Fezziwig rubs his hands, loosens his clothing, laughs, and has a "rich, fat, jovial voice". He behaves warmly towards his apprentices (Scrooge and Dick Wilkins), who move everything out of the way for the office party, reinventing it as a "snug, and warm, and dry, and bright…ball-room". There is a violinist, and Fezziwig's wife, three daughters, all of his employees and domestic servants, and their guests, and the neighbours and near neighbours; forty or more people altogether, with a buffet of meat, mice pies and beer. Fezziwig has a physical grace- he skips, dances, emits light (like the Ghost of Christmas Past- to show Scrooge how things should be done) and acts the perfect host, before the party- a "domestic ball"- ends after four hours at 11 p.m., with him shaking hands with every single guest and wishing them a Merry Christmas individually.

The Ghost and Scrooge then discuss the value of money- a little ("three or four…..pounds of your mortal money") generates much more happiness in its use than in its not being spent; and Scrooge begins to see that it is better to speak warmly and generously to your employees than to complain and resent their Christmas day at home, as he had, in sending Bob home.

This scene focuses on two things- Fezziwig's generosity as an employer and a host (however faint the social connection with his guests, the invitation is to an open house), and the transformative power of extending the hand of friendship- you become happy by helping others to be happy. Most of the guests are poor (housemaid, baker, cook, milkman, the boy…..suspected of not having enough board); they are people without money of their own, but they are not, as Scrooge claims, of no interest, value or dignity ("These silly folks").

Even those who have transgressed- the girl who had "had her ears pulled by her mistress", and, earlier, the tailor who had been fined for being drunk and disorderly- deserve a Christmas which relieves them of their troubles, and overlooks their wrongdoing.

Fezziwig stands as Scrooge's first employer and someone who showed him kindness when he benefited from it; Scrooge understands now that he should do the same to

Bob Cratchit, but Fezziwig's role as a facilitator of fun for the poor in the wider community around him is a step beyond Scrooge at this stage. Whereas Belle serves to show Scrooge what he has lost, by never having it, Fezziwig, like Marley, serves to show him what he can and should do.

Fred

Scrooge's nephew is the antithesis of his uncle. Fred is always generous in spirit, inclined to give, not to take, and disposed to think the best of others, excusing their crabbiness or narrow-mindedness. With his energy and enthusiasm, he takes Scrooge by surprise, and greets him in "a cheerful voice". His glowing ruddy complexion, sparkling eyes and general vigour generate heat- but not enough to melt Scrooge's coldness.

Fred's approach, in the opening scene, anticipates both the Ghost of Christmas Present (in his emphasis on kindness and goodwill among all people) and the reformed or "reclaimed" version of Scrooge, who will, like Fred, come to see Christmas as "a good time: a kind, forgiving, charitable, pleasant time". Here, though, Scrooge tells him he would rather go to Hell than accept the invitation to Christmas

Dinner at Fred's. Fred allows Scrooge his hostility, but he refuses to be discouraged, saying that he has made the offer (or "trial") "in homage to Christmas"- extending the hand of hospitality and friendship even where it is rejected for no sensible reason.

Rather like Fezziwig (and unlike Scrooge), Fred presides over Christmas at home, merrily ("Ha, ha!" laughed Scrooge's nephew. "Ha, ha, ha!"), and his wife and guests cannot stop laughing- at the idea, as it turns out, that Scrooge "said that Christmas was a humbug".

Fred's house is "bright, dry, gleaming"; his wife "pretty....a ripe little mouth...the sunniest pair of eyes". This is the personification of lively goodwill, and, just like Bob, Fred will not criticise Scrooge. He explains that he feels sorry for Scrooge, who is denying himself a little pleasure and entertainment- but he will keep on inviting him every Christmas, however often Scrooge continues to be obstinate and humourless.

The women here are like Mrs Cratchit- and this is not just Mrs Fred, but also her "sisters, and all the other ladies"- in being critical of Scrooge. They are like the Ghosts, Belle and Mrs Cratchit, in seeing Scrooge's lack of empathy and humanity as not just a harmless weakness, but a sin- a moral offence- because men who can make money should establish a home and family, make it comfortable, and support others who are trying to do the same. Fred's wife is intelligent, and the other women "sharp"; her "plump sister" works out that, in the game of yes and no, Scrooge is being described (by Fred) as "an animal…..disagreeable…..savage"; some of the women say Fred should have accepted the suggestion that Scrooge was, in fact, a bear- a lumbering (sub-human) creature which arouses a kind of horrified fascination.

The reformed Scrooge visits Fred; the time-travelling clock of the narrative is turned back, and they now have the Christmas Fred had offered him in the first place, as this is reality, rather than the virtual reality of the trip with the Ghost of Christmas Present's tableau.

Although he had only met Bob Cratchit once or twice (presumably including his visit to Scrooge at work at the start of the tale) Fred has been sensitive and shown "extraordinary kindness" over the apparent death of Tiny Tim, offering any help they might need- "giving me his card"- where, of course, Scrooge had refused the cards of the charity collectors. What struck Bob was not Fred's offer to help financially but his empathy ("It really seemed as if he…..felt with us"). Scrooge can only learn from the contrast, and he does.

Belle

Immediately after seeing Fezziwig- who exposes to Scrooge his social and civic inadequacies as an entrepreneur, and shows him what he can and should do- he is forced to face Belle, his former fiancée, and confront what he has lost and cannot now have- domestic happiness and a family of his own.

She rejects him, because his love of money has grown stronger than his love of her. The adjectives which describe him here ("eager, greedy, restless") show that she is right- we might say that he is possessed by the Spirit of Avarice.

Dickens even uses the New Testament noun "root" (as in "the love of money is the root of all evil") to generate the image of a tree- we can see where its shadow will fall, when it has grown to maturity; that is, when Scrooge has gone beyond "the prime of life" to his present declining years.

Belle is crying, and wearing "a mourning-dress", as if their love is a person who has died, not an emotion. Like Fred, she does not judge or reprimand Scrooge. She gives a measured analysis. When they were first engaged, they were both poor, and, like many young couples, they anticipated gradually improving their financial security. However, Scrooge became gripped by the fear of poverty, so that his interests went on to become the narrow and exclusive pursuit of wealth. Indeed, as a money lender, he achieves his own financial security by preying on the poverty of others.

As the scene changes to Belle's home, with her husband, daughter and various younger children, Scrooge has to consider whether the pursuit of money has made him happier than having a family would have done, especially now that he is "in the haggard winter of his life." On the very day of Marley's death- a day, Christmas Eve, seven years earlier than the scene Scrooge now watches, and when he had continued to transact business, instead of mourning Marley- Scrooge's isolation and friendlessness is a source of amusement to them, because they have created a family (children again) and Scrooge has created nothing more than a bank balance.

Narrative structure- the scenes

The tale is called "A Christmas Carol. Being a Ghost Story of Christmas" and it has a short preface in which Dickens makes it clear that it is designed as a comedy- "this Ghostly little book………..raise the Ghost of an Idea……not put my readers out of humour……may it haunt their house pleasantly, and no one wish to lay it".

Instead of using chapters, it is written in five "staves"- like the words and music of a Christmas song or carol. It has some music in it- a carol sung through the keyhole of Scrooge's office, Fezziwig's violin-accompanied dancing, and the musical party at Fred's house.

In understanding the structure of the novella it is more helpful to think in terms of the individual scenes, rather than the "staves". Several short scenes take place within each stave, and there are 21 separate scenes in total. The shortness and variety in the scenes, linked by the device of the Spirits leading Scrooge through his past, present and future, is the key to the ease with which the novella transfers to the theatre.

It is important for you to have a clear sense of the sequence of the scenes. Here they are-

Stave 1

Scene 1

Scrooge in his counting house at 3 p.m. on Christmas Eve; he is visited by Fred, by the two gentlemen collecting money for the poor, and he and Bob leave the office for Christmas. It is the seventh anniversary of Marley's death.

Scene 2

Scrooge goes home, and sees Marley's face in the door knocker. Then Marley's ghost appears in Scrooge's room, explains that Scrooge has "a chance and a hope of escaping my fate" and will be "haunted by Three Spirits"- the first at 1 a.m., the second on the next night at 1 a.m., and the third at midnight at the end of December 26th- a period of 35 hours in total. The ghost vanishes by jumping out of the window. Scrooge shuts the window and goes to sleep. It is after 2 a.m. on Christmas Day.

Stave 2

Scene 3

Scrooge wakes up as the clocks strike 12 midnight. He has gone back in time; when the clocks strike 1 a.m., the Ghost of Christmas Past arrives and explains that his visit is to improve Scrooge's "welfare" and that they need to "walk" together.

Scene 4

Scrooge is transported to the countryside and his boyhood self, in "a little market-town". He is shown himself, at school, where he is alone, reading, in the Christmas school holidays; then, a few years later, his "much younger" sister (Fan) comes to the school to say he is being allowed home.

Scene 5

The ghost shows Scrooge the Christmas party when he was Fezziwig's apprentice.

Scene 6

Scrooge sees himself being rejected by his fiancée, who criticises him for his devotion to money. This is after his apprenticeship. He is probably in his early thirties, and beginning to make money as a money lender to the poor.

Scene 7

The Ghost "pinions" him and forces him to see the life he could have had- the domestic happiness of a family with children of his own, instead of which he is known only for being "quite alone in the world"- without a family or friends. At the end of this scene, Scrooge finds himself back in bed at home; he falls asleep.

Stave 3

Scene 8

Scrooge wakes up; again, it is just before 1 a.m. The Ghost of Christmas Present does not come after 15 minutes- because it is already in the room next door, which is much altered, with a Christmas feast laid out. The Ghost makes this vanish, and transports Scrooge to Christmas morning, outside.

Scene 9

The street scene is described in three and a half pages of detail, focusing on the habits of the poor.

Scene 10

Scrooge observes the Cratchit household on Christmas Day; this is a six-page set piece.

Scene 11

The ghost takes Scrooge, briefly, to see the Christmas customs of a mining community, lighthouse keepers, and a ship's crew.

Scene 12

Christmas at Scrooge's nephew's house (over almost 6 pages). Scrooge is criticised, as he was in Belle's house and by Mrs Cratchit (but not at Fezziwig's, where he was too young to be able to improve Christmas for others, but should have learned from the generosity Fezziwig showed him).

Scene 13

Stave 3 closes with a summary of the extended tour with the Ghost which lasts until Twelfth Night (January 6th) and includes visits to "sick beds…..foreign lands…..struggling men…..poverty….alms-house, hospital, and jail…..a children's party". Having shown Scrooge the importance of seeking out and attacking and easing poverty, the ghost confronts him with the allegorical figures of Want and Ignorance in the form of a feral boy and girl. The Ghost must depart at midnight, after quoting Scrooge's own anti-social words from Stave 1. As the Ghost of Christmas Present disappears, the Ghost of Christmas Yet To Come approaches Scrooge.

Stave 4

Scene 14

The Ghost shows Scrooge his fellow merchants at the Exchange, two of his associates in the street, and a commercial centre where "another man stood in his accustomed corner"; Scrooge is absent, and spoken of as dead, but not mourned for.

Scene 15

At old Joe's shop, the undertaker and the two women- the laundress and the charwoman- sell the personal effects of a dead man, whom Scrooge does not yet recognise as himself.

Scene 16

A deathbed; the Phantom wants Scrooge to identify the corpse, but he cannot bring himself to do so.

Scene 17

The Ghost answers Scrooge's request to see "any person…who feels emotion caused by this man's death" by showing him the mother (Caroline) and her husband, for whom the death (Scrooge's) is a release from the inability to pay a debt on time. Scrooge would hope to be mourned; not for his death to be celebrated and a relief to people he came into contact with.

Scene 18

When Scrooge revises his request, so that it becomes "let me see some tenderness connected with a death", the

Ghost takes him to the Cratchits to see that Tiny Tim has died.

Scene 19

The Ghost shows Scrooge to see a tombstone, and he can no longer deny that the recently deceased man whom no-one would miss, grieve for, or even speak of by name was him. The scene- and Stave 4- ends with the phantom's hand shaking, as a sign to Scrooge that this vision of the post-Scrooge world- in which he had done as little as Marley, and would be condemned to the same restless fate- is still avoidable.

Stave 5

Scene 20

Scrooge awakes on Christmas morning, free of the ghosts; he gets up, orders that the biggest turkey is sent to the Cratchits, and goes out to greet people on the streets, make up for his meanness to the two portly gentlemen, and attend church. Then he visits Fred (having refused to at the start of Stave 1); now he is a participant, not an observer, in the "wonderful happiness".

Scene 21

At 9.18 am on Boxing Day he makes amends with Bob, by raising his salary, and telling him to have a warmer office fire.

This structure departs from Dickens' usual method, which is to tell a story chronologically- as we expect from a novel. Scrooge recedes as a character, as the various scenes or tableaux become longer, later in the novella. In Stave 4, Scrooge is slow to recognise that he is being shown the world after he has died, and there is dramatic irony here; the reader knows what he does not. Normally, we associate dramatic irony with tragedy, but in this case we know- partly from Dickens' own preface- that this story is neither a horror story nor a tragedy, but a celebration of the possibility of redemption or "reclamation", as Scrooge reinvents himself, from misanthrope to philanthropist.

Scrooge recedes in importance, because the Ghosts progressively engage him less and less in conversation. We may expect the hero in a novel to embark on a quest or a journey of growing up which will keep them firmly at the centre of the action ("Jane Eyre", "Emma", and Dickens' own "Great Expectations" all do this). Scrooge, by contrast, regresses; it is as if the ghosts subject him to a session of psychotherapy in which he faces the memories he has repressed, and uses that cathartic process to change his behaviour. In that sense, the action of the novella really only begins as the written story ends- just as scrooge's new life starts once he has put the old one aside.

Dickens' use of comedy

The preface contains a humorous comment; Dickens says that his ghost story is not intended to haunt the reader unpleasantly, or put anyone "out of humour" with anyone else. From the outset, it is clear that we are not to be frightened, and one of the ways Dickens ensures this is though his use of humour.

The narrator calls on the precedent of the ghost of Hamlet's father in Shakespeare's "Hamlet"- a dramatic/literary ghost, not a real one. Marley's ghost comes to save Scrooge, not to haunt him, and the three Spirits want to show him a better way, not haunt him into some type of madness.

The narrator is a man with a sense of humour, although we may find it slightly grating. He always has a word of appreciation for a pretty girl.

At Fred's house, Topper is a young man whose only purpose in the story is to raise a smile from the reader. Fred himself can barely open his mouth without laughing, and the Spirit of Christmas Present is a jovial, Santa Claus figure- a celebrator of the excesses of overeating and overdrinking in a festive season where care is laid aside and where he dispenses good cheer with his wand, which dissolves conflict.

Dickens likes to describe children in safe families as energetic and anarchic (far from the Victorian saying that they should be "seen and not heard"). Belle's children and the young Cratchits are like this, and so are the boys at Scrooge's school. Fezziwig, Fred and finally Scrooge himself are all presented as children in adults' bodies, with their enthusiasm, energy and lack of poise and seriousness. Scrooge even becomes a practical joker when he pretends he is about to sack Bob before awarding him a pay rise. There is joking between Scrooge and Marley's ghost; can a ghost sit on a chair or not?

If we took out the aspect of comedy the novella would be much darker and less cheerful. The visit of Marley's ghost, the appearance of Ignorance and Want at the end of Stave

3, and the whole of Stave 4, dominated by Scrooge's possible legacy of futility and the prospect of Tiny Tim's dying (with the implication that Scrooge will be damned for failing to save him), are all dark in tone. Scrooge's memories of his schooldays and of being rejected by Belle are painful. Dickens needs to inject the comedy and humour to give the tale enough zest and humanity so that it is a celebration of the possibilities of Christmas, rather than a dry morality tale about the redemption of the sinner Scrooge.

Dickens' use of pathos

Victorian writers often use pathos- the technique of making the reader feel sad on behalf of a character. This is particularly common when some moral point is being made- perhaps about social injustice. It is there in Blake's "Songs of Innocence and Experience", as early as 1789.

In "A Christmas Carol", Dickens uses pathos to direct our empathy for the Cratchits, for Scrooge, and for the poor in general, and particularly for poor children.

Tiny Tim is feeble, weak, and in grave danger of dying; his remorseless gratitude, cheerfulness and refusal to feel sorry for himself makes him a little hero, and enables the

Ghost of Christmas Present to lecture Scrooge on the immorality of judging one life as worth less than another.

Having presented and established Scrooge as a thoroughly unlikeable character at the outset, Dickens creates a sense of pathos over his abandonment, as a boy, at school, away from his family, and again over his own reaction to his rejection by Belle. Somewhere inside Scrooge there is still the child whose imagination warmed to stories and who was friends with children his own age. This glimmer of warmth, buried under glaciers of entrenched personal unhappiness, is the spark which ignites our sympathy for Scrooge; he becomes an underdog and we want his reformation to succeed.

The description of the Cratchits' Christmas, and Bob's uncomplaining decency and tenderness in the teeth of acute financial insecurity, makes us empathise with them too. Mrs Cratchit is less sympathetic to the reader, because she is resentful of Scrooge's meanness. This is understandable from her point of view, as a mother struggling to keep her family out of the workhouse, but we admire Bob's patient suffering more than her impatient suffering.

The description of Ignorance and Want is intended to shock. It is allegorical, in presenting the two children as "monsters" lurking where there should be angels, not devils, and "mysteries of wonderful creation"- a warning of the real possibility of a revolution and social upheaval if Scrooge's attitude, that the workhouses and prisons are enough to deal with the problem of poverty, prevails.

There is no pathos attached to the prospective death of the unredeemed Scrooge; just as he has preyed on others (the debtor Caroline and her family), his corpse will be preyed upon by Mrs Dilber and her associates. Dickens has no sympathy for adults who make bad moral decisions (we are not asked to feel sorry for Marley's ghost) but innocent children who are starved of education and humane employment are victims who deserve a better way of life.

The gothic element

The gothic genre in literature originates in 1764 with Horace Walpole's novel "The Castle of Otranto". It developed into a literary form which combined romance, death and horror- Mary Shelley's "Frankenstein" (1818) and Bram Stoker's "Dracula" (1897) are gothic novels, and Keats's poems "La belle dame sans merci" (1819) and "Isabella" (1820) are romantic horror tales.

While critics looked down on the conventions of gothic writing, it was very popular in England in the 1840s and 1850s. Dickens was always aware of popular literary tastes, and even in "Great Expectations" (1860-61), a novel of an entirely different sort, there is a gothic episode. Even in the late Victorian era, Robert Louis Stevenson's "Strange Case of Dr Jekyll and Mr Hyde" (1886) and Oscar Wilde's "The Picture of Dorian Gray" (1891) are laced with gothic elements as well as- more seriously- testing the concept of the limits of individual freedom and social responsibility.

Dickens' ghost story therefore satisfies a hunger in the reading market for the supernatural; but where a writer such as Edgar Allan Poe would use it to evoke sensations of fear in the reader, Dickens' ghosts are not frightening or sinister; they are comical, and they haunt, not to destroy Scrooge's sanity, but to save his soul from purgatory.

Scrooge himself "was not much in the habit of cracking jokes", but, partly through the interventions of the narrator, and partly through the narrative style, the gothic aspects contribute to the comedy- especially when Scrooge is talking to Marley's ghost. In Stave 4, however, it suits Dickens to take the gothic style more literally and seriously; the fact that the Ghost of Christmas Yet To Come is invisible under a black cloak, and utterly silent, reinforces the grave and sombre atmosphere as Scrooge is forced to contemplate his own death. The contrast in Stave 5, when Scrooge bursts into the Christmas morning sunshine, and into "golden sunlight…..sweet fresh air", and a new world of happiness and light, is all the stronger because the preceding episode has been so dark in colour and character. When he sends the turkey to Bob Cratchit's, his hand quivers, just as the final phantom's had, as it conceded, wordlessly, that Scrooge can save himself after all. In the end, the ghosts are all committed to "reclaiming" Scrooge by showing him his "Ignorance" about the poor- and his prejudices about Christmas.

Poverty in the 1840s.

The welfare state in its present form- based on a socially accepted principle that there is a basic poverty line below which no-one should fall- is less than a century old.

No such safety net existed in the 19th century. Until the end of the 18th century it had been accepted that landowners- who were much richer than the working class- should support the poorest and most ill people in their parish or locality.

The Napoleonic Wars ended in 1815 and the cost of supporting the poor had almost doubled between 1803 and 1818. A debate had developed (rather like the one we have today among Members of Parliament over how to "make work pay"). Some political economists argued that if the poor were entitled to fixed relief or benefits this would interfere with the setting of wages; it was fairer if there was a free market economy in which wages were higher where labour was scarce, and vice versa.

In his 1798 pamphlet "Principles of Population" Thomas Malthus had argued that the poor laws actually encouraged poverty and kept the poor in poverty; the poor would have larger families because they knew they would have a guaranteed level of financial support. Those enlarged families would have no prospect of escaping poverty.

In 1816 a committee of Parliament called for landowners to have the right to support the poor locally at rates of their own choosing, to combat the sharp rise in the overall costs of statutory support. In the 1820s an experiment was conducted in Nottinghamshire. Deterrent workhouses were compulsory for people who claimed relief; conditions were harsh and families were broken up. Unsurprisingly, the cost of providing for the poor came down.

The number of people entitled to elect MPs doubled (to about I million) in 1832 and it became politically expedient to cut the bill for the poor further. In 1834 a new Poor Law came into force. Although it tried to make financial support conditional on accepting the very harsh conditions of life in the workhouse, this proved not to be practicable; in 1841, there were just under 200000 people in workhouses and

1.1 million received poverty relief while living in their own homes.

The economic benefits of the Industrial Revolution were not felt until some time after 1843. Dickens' own family had been affected by poverty. His father, like Bob Cratchit, was a clerk with a growing family which was, perhaps, familiar with the pawnbrokers ie living on the poverty line; unlike Bob, he went to prison for three months in 1824 for non-payment of debts, and Charles Dickens, at the age of 12, was expected to support his family by earning six shillings per week working in a factory.

In 1842, a "ragged school" was set up in Field Lane in London, to offer the most basic education to poor children (again, an equivalent appears in "Great Expectations") without any process of selection. Dickens visited it. From 1842, a series of reports by the Children's Employment Commission documented the dangerous working conditions to which children were exposed in mines and manufacturing. Dickens' mother had attempted to set up a school of her own in London, but she could not attract a single pupil.

We should not be surprised that, having experienced the disruptive, anti-family effects of debt as a 12-year-old, and observing the chronic lack of hope for uneducated children in London as an adult, Dickens then invented the allegorical children Ignorance and Want, and made the need to act against child poverty the central thesis of "A Christmas Carol" in 1843. Dickens, having had his own education ended suddenly at the age of 12, will have seen a decent education as the best means of escaping a life of poverty and crime. Even so, he felt that the ragged schools were too religious in character to be an effective solution, although they did keep some potentially criminal children out of trouble, to some extent.

It is therefore sensible to argue that, at its heart, "A Christmas Carol" is really a critique of the lack of funding and opportunity for the children of the poor; they need a proper education, without excessively strong religious overtones, in order to navigate their way out of absolute poverty. This education should be funded, in the society Dickens lived in, not by landowners but by the increasingly prosperous metropolitan middle class- Scrooge, Marley and their business associates.

Dickens' claim that "A Christmas Carol" is a slight tale about Christmas is a little misleading. As he wrote it, he knew that it would have greater reach and power than any political or reforming pamphlet he might write about the plight of working children. And in fact the novella had a striking effect on some business people; there were tales of employers in both Britain and the USA (where Dickens' popularity was immense) giving their workers time off at Christmas, and even the gift of a turkey, in imitation of Fezziwig, Scrooge and the Ghost of Christmas Present!

Scrooge's Timeline

A word about timescales. The Christmas Eve on which Marley's ghost appears is the seventh anniversary of his death. Let's assume that Scrooge is aged 60 and that he and Marley were identical in age, as they were in so many other ways. If the story is set in 1843 (there is no indication that it is not) Scrooge would have been born in 1783. Apprenticeships theoretically took children from the age of 14 to 21, so Fezziwig's party may have been in about 1800.

Scrooge was engaged to Belle when they were both poor, and when they were starting on their working lives- so perhaps in about 1805. When Belle breaks the engagement, Scrooge is "older now; a man in the prime of life. His face had not the harsh and rigid lines of later years; but it had begun to wear the signs of care and avarice". Moreover, until 1823, the minimum legal age for marrying was 21; engagements normally lasted for up to two years. Scrooge may not have been financially secure enough to marry the dowry-less Belle for much longer than this; nor may he have seen her as much of a financial asset. A woman like Belle would hope to be married by the age of about 30, and indeed she becomes "a comely matron" with more children than Scrooge could count. Yet Belle's husband announces that Marley is about to die; so we can date this episode to 1836, when Belle is perhaps 50. If Belle's oldest child was about as old as Martha Cratchit, Belle may have married- securely, it seems- in about 1816; probably at the age of about 30.

Understanding this timeline dramatizes the stark choice Scrooge made. He has spent the past thirty years making money, which, as Fred says, he merely accumulates, and does nothing with, while Belle and the Cratchits have established happy and lasting families as a richer legacy of their lives.

Sample Essays

These are both structured to fit the time scales for Edexcel candidates. As such, you would have around 50 minutes to write the following. If you are sitting a different exam board, please see the notes at the end.

Essay Question 1

A pale light, rising in the outer air, fell straight upon the bed; and on it, plundered and bereft, unwatched, unwept, uncared for, was the body of this man. (2)

Scrooge glanced towards the Phantom. Its steady hand was pointed to the head. The cover was so carelessly adjusted that the slightest raising of it, the motion of a finger upon Scrooge's part, would have disclosed the face. He thought of it, felt how easy it would be to do, and longed to do it; but had no more power to withdraw the veil than to dismiss the spectre at his side. (6)

Oh, cold, cold, rigid, dreadful Death, set up thine altar here, and dress it with such terrors as thou hast at thy command; for this is thy dominion! But of the loved, revered, and honoured head, thou canst not turn one hair to thy dread purposes, or make one feature odious. It is not that the hand is heavy and will fall down when released; it is not that the heart and pulse are still; but that the hand WAS open, generous and true; the heart brave, warm, and tender; and the pulse a man's. Strike, Shadow, strike! And see his good deeds springing from the wound, to sow the world with life immortal! (13)

No voice pronounced these words in Scrooge's ears, and yet he heard them when he looked upon the bed. (15)

Starting with this extract, how does Dickens present life and death?

Write about:

- How Dickens presents life and death in this extract
- How Dickens presents life and death in the novel as a whole.

Answer

This is a moment of dramatic irony, where Scrooge still cannot bring himself to concede that the unloved corpse is his own. The Phantom has an authoritative hand, which it uses to point Scrooge in several uncomfortable directions, to different places, in Stave 4; Scrooge is not yet ready to face the potential for his own death (and his own life) to be meaningless. Using the finger of his own hand, he could confront the issue of the corpse, lift its shroud and identify it, but he has to be shown his own potential grave instead, at the end of Stave 4, before he can resolve to lay his old life and attitudes to rest.

The novella dramatizes, in the form of a gothic but humorous ghost story, the philosophical question of what a good life is. Marley, Belle and the three Christmas Ghosts agree that the love and pursuit of money ("Gain") will leave us unmourned for, and the capacity for good which we all have in our lives unrealised. The three "un"- adjectives in line 2 dramatise the wasted potential for doing good, which Marley's ghost had explained to Scrooge was the consequence of being materialistic and insular.

The lexis of death here (veil, spectre, cold, rigid, dreadful Death, terrors, dread, odious, Shadow, wound) contrasts with the opposite thesis- that the good deeds we do can make us immortal because of what we "sow" (we reap what we sow is a Biblical idea) and mitigate the awfulness of dying.

The "pale light" in line 1 indicates that there is an opportunity for enlightenment or the discovery of truth here, but that it will not be grasped; the Ghosts of the Past and Present emit strong, bright light when they deliver lessons and truths to Scrooge and he understands them. Much of Stave 4 is dark in tone because it is dealing with the future legacy of Scrooge's unaltered life, and the possible death of Tiny Tim, who, Scrooge has come to understand, is not surplus to the population after all.

The change in register or tone in line 7 is dramatic, gothic and rhetorical, with its frequent imperatives, its direct address to Death, the force of its lament, and its apparent concession that Death holds the upper hand (that we should worship at the altar of Death is a grotesque idea). However, the triplet of love, reverence and honour (three abstract nouns), secured by good deeds, confers immortal life of a sort.

The imagery of hands is striking. A slack hand (like Marley's ghost's slack jaw) is a proof of death, and of the inability to do anything, as is the absence of a pulse, and a still heart; but a good man's hand "WAS" (note the emphasis- this is the only instance of capitalisation in the whole text) "open, generous, and true"- like the hand of the Ghost of Christmas Present. This type of hand foreshadows Scrooge's financial largesse in Stave 5 and it understands the fight against poverty, Ignorance and Want.

The Ghost of Christmas Yet

To Come never speaks a word; Scrooge is now answering his own questions, through an internal voice, because he has reached a proper understanding of the need for benevolence as a redemptive or reclamatory force.

The bed (lines 1 and 15) is a simple symbol for death. Scrooge's paralysis- he cannot lift the sheet to recognise himself as he has been in his life up till now- creates a space in which the rhetorical third paragraph can articulate Scrooge's own thought process. He concludes that it is better to be remembered warmly for good deeds than to be one of the ghosts Marley is among- unable to intervene for anyone's welfare. Scrooge's practical help for the Cratchits (the huge turkey instead of the smallish goose, and Bob's pay rise, and ongoing financial help) will save Tiny Tim, as well as saving Scrooge.

The language of the extract alludes to the Church and the Bible, to give it moral seriousness; but Dickens presents helping the poor as a social duty, not a religious obligation. Scrooge attends church on Christmas Day in the closing pages, but he is not a religious man- he is rational and sceptical, but the ghosts have proved to him that it is better to be a Fezziwig or a Fred than the old kind of Scrooge.

Scrooge is an archetype of the neglectful, self-made, monied class- and he is socially bankrupt (unmourned and friendless) in his corpse form here. The five hard, cold adjectives in the opening sentence reflect the character of the old, flint-like Scrooge, and the deictic definition of "this man" is delayed, tellingly, to the end of the sentence. Scrooge resists the idea of dying in this character he has been until now; his inner voice now features the words "generous" and "good deeds", which were alien to him when he turned the portly gentlemen away empty-handed in the opening scene.

Essay Question 2

And now Scrooge looked on more attentively than ever, when the master of the house, having his daughter leaning fondly on him, sat down with her and her mother at his own fireside; and when he thought that such another creature, quite as graceful and as full of promise, might have called him father, and been a spring-time in the haggard winter of his life, his sight grew very dim indeed. (4)

"Belle", said the husband, turning to his wife with a smile, "I saw an old friend of yours this afternoon."

"Who was it?"

"Guess!" (8)

"How can I? Tut, don't I know," she added in the same breath, laughing as he laughed. "Mr Scrooge."

"Mr Scrooge it was. I passed his office window; and as it was not shut up, and he had a candle inside, I could scarcely help seeing him. His partner lies on the point of death, I hear; and there he sat alone. Quite alone in the world, I do believe." (12)

Starting with this extract, how does Dickens present family as a positive force for good?

Write about:

- How Dickens presents family in this extract
- How Dickens presents family as a positive force for good in the novel as a whole

Answer

Throughout the novella, Dickens maintains a sense that being successful in business is more or less incompatible with having a happy home life and marriage. Scrooge and Marley are kindred spirits, and Marley had "no bowels" or tenderness. None of Scrooge's business associates seem to be married and none of the ghosts among whom Marley belongs is female. Bob Cratchit's tender heart, as well as his poverty, may make it impossible for him ever to be his own boss; he is not ruthless enough.

Stave 2 is about Christmas Past. Scrooge evidently grew up in a family which sent him away to boarding school and never had him home for long periods, so that he had to try to keep loneliness and social isolation at bay. Characters in books (like Ali Baba and Robinson Crusoe) had to take the place of the friends he could not have in the real world, and he had no experience of emotional closeness except to his much younger sister. We understand, therefore, why his engagement to Belle failed; not only because of his growing attachment to money but perhaps also because he was uncomfortable with intimacy.

It is daring to end Stave 2 with a depiction of the life Scrooge could have had, if he had valued money less and emotional "welfare" more. The worst consequence of not marrying is the being "quite alone in the world". The connotation of coldness and winter is of Scrooge's anti-social character, but the striking "haggard winter of his life" is one of Dickens' nods to Shakespeare, and specifically to the opening line of "Richard 3rd"- "now is the winter of our discontent". Winter, loneliness and coldness have a cluster of meanings, and Scrooge is becoming painfully aware of how emotionally cold his life remains in mature adulthood, because when he was younger he had thrown away his only chance of marrying and having a family of his own.

Three extended scenes in the novella present domestic married life, at least under the stimulus of Christmas festivities, as a constant stream of fun, noise, laughter and happiness- at the Cratchits', Fred's, and at Fezziwig's.

Fezziwig is the benevolent, generous man of means whom, through his apprenticeship, Scrooge should have learnt from. He should have modelled himself on his first employer, who had been so kind to him.

The end of Stave 1 sees Scrooge, alone, "double-locked" in his isolation; the end of Stave 2, alone again, in his bedroom, emotionally exhausted and inadequate; the end of Stave 3 sees his transfer from one phantom to another; the end of Stave 4 has Scrooge saying his goodbye to the last of the ghosts. Scrooge's only meaningful conversations are with the ghosts, until the final sentences of the novella, which promise that he will now start to have a proper dialogue with Bob, after all these years. Scrooge will finally escape the curse of loneliness, but only by the narrowest margin. In telling Bob to have a larger fire, Scrooge is introducing some sorely needed physical (and emotional) warmth into their relationship, and taking it beyond its previously cold and distant connection in business only.

Fezziwig is a role model for the sort of entrepreneurship Dickens advocates; he is generous with his money, and treats people of all classes and occupations as though they were members of his own family.

Scrooge finally comes to appreciate Fred's hospitality both from the outside, observing it, and then participating in it; when he becomes "a second father" to Tiny Tim, he acquires a family of a kind. In the novella, being unmarried reinforces your rough edges and ill humour; no-one with a family and children is misanthropic in the novella, except for Scrooge's own (unseen) father.

This is not an accurate representation of real life, but the novella shows us social intercourse as a way of promoting cohesion and resilience; people who interact positively with other people at home go on to spread goodwill in the wider community outside (Fred). By contrast, Marley's spiritual bankruptcy (and, by extension, that of his business partner, Scrooge) originated in his failure to set foot in the community "beyond our counting-house……..our money-changing hole".

There are no arguments in Fred's household, or Bob's, or Fezziwig's, or Belle's- only laughter, and the freedom to be like a child. The only dysfunctional family is the one Scrooge did not himself grow up in as a boy.

Notes for Edexcel Candidates

Remember, whilst you are advised to spend 55 minutes on "A Christmas Carol" your question will be split into two

First, is an extract in which you will be invited to "explore how Dickens presents" a character or theme   then for the remainder of the time you will be asked to explain how that theme or character appears in the novel as a whole.

 from the text, and writing in a suitable critical style (AO1); and for analysing how language, form and structure create

Notes for WJEC Candidates

The novella is an option in Unit 2b. Here you will have an hour to answer a question in two parts- a twenty minute

About your exam—final tips for success

You'll have seen in the sample essays that what counts is organising what you want to say (you must list and then prioritise your points, in order of importance, in a plan) and then saying it, clearly and concisely.

You can be sure that the questions in your exam will be fair; they are designed to let you show how well you understand the set text, and how you respond to it- not to catch you out. The examiner wants to "mark you in" and will reward you for a thoughtful response which answers the question directly. Don't try to write down everything you have to say. If the essay is on a particular character or theme, stick to that- the quality of your thoughts will still shine through.

Whatever exam board you are with, look on its website. Not just at the questions on past and specimen papers- you must also pay close attention to the mark schemes AND the comments in the examiners' reports. Don't be shy to raise this with your teachers- they will be happy to spend time in class covering these vital aspects of succeeding in your exam. Ask your teachers to go through the marking criteria; make sure that you know how to get the best possible mark- that is, what you will get marks for, and what you won't.

And a pitfall to avoid

Don't fall into the trap of having a list of quotations you're determined to force into any essay. If you know the book- and, surely, by now, you must do!!- suitable short references will pop into your mind when you need them.

Your number one focus is on answering the question in front of you.

Your number two focus is exactly the same.

So is focus number three.

We could go on!!

Answering the question means taking it apart and highlighting the key words (often that little word "how"); then making a proper plan, which organises your material, gives you an argument, and leads you to a clear and convincing conclusion; writing your essay from the plan; and stopping as soon as you get to the end of what you planned to say. Don't add a bit more for the sake of it- you will only lose time, marks and structural clarity when you should be going on to the next question in the exam.

A proper essay plan leads to an essay that needs nothing added after its conclusion, because all your points were in your plan to begin with.

Please, please resist the temptation to start writing your answer straight after you've read the question, even if most of the other people in your exam do just that. The exam allows you time to plan your answer. Make sure you use it for that purpose.

Check every sentence you write, or want to write, against what the question asks you to do. If what you are writing doesn't answer the question, leave it out, and write something that does.

Especially if you are taking your GCSE this summer, I wish you every success. Remember that if you're really stuck and your teachers can't help you, you can contact the author- grnsmithers@hotmail.co.uk. Just don't leave it till the night before the exam!

Printed in Great Britain
by Amazon